LOUISE

MY STORY

LOUISE
MY STORY

KATE THORNTON & JANE PRESTON

Virgin

the early years

It's June 1988, 1 a.m. Inside the stark, whitewashed interior of Soho's trendiest club, a man stands at the bar surveying the pandemonium on the dance floor. In the middle of the throng of sweaty bodies, all moving in time to the beat, he catches sight of a lush young woman. He gulps his drink and takes in her energetic, grinding gyrations, watching with amusement as a crowd slowly gathers around her. He makes his way through the crowd for a closer inspection, his eyes trained upon her: her golden skin, blue Bambi eyes and a smile straight from an American toothpaste ad. Fumbling in his jacket, he pulls out a business card and taps the girl on the shoulder.

Louise and her mum, Lynne.

'Can you sing as well as you dance?' he asks.

'Yeah, of course I can,' she replies, with a confidence that will serve her well in years to come.

'I'm Denis Ingoldsby. I'm a manager, and I'm looking for young, female singers. If you really can sing, call me,' he says, giving her the card. 'So, what's your name?'

'Louise,' she says, viewing him cautiously.

'Well, Louise,' he says, 'let me tell you, one day you could be as big as Madonna.'

'From the moment she could walk, she was forever dressing up and singing and dancing. She was performing before she could string a sentence together,' says Louise's mum, Lynne Nurding. 'Her dad, Tim, is a huge Motown fan, so Stevie Wonder and Smokey Robinson records were constantly blasting out of the stereo. She'd pretend her hairbrush was a microphone and stand in front of the mirror for hours belting out songs, lost in a world of her own. The noise used to drive me mad. I'd constantly be turning the music down, but as soon as my back was turned, Louise, or her dad, would turn the volume back up full-blast. She was in training for this – her success – from the moment she could walk.

'She was a lovely little girl, always cared about other people. She could be a real little worrier at times. She was an only child until she was twelve, but when her brothers Samuel and Joseph were born she loved helping out and mothering them. We always got asked back twice wherever we went with Louise, adults loved her. Unlike the boys, who you can't take anywhere. As long as Lou had her Sindy suitcase, complete with doll and a few clothes, then she'd sit on the floor

'From the moment she could walk, she was forever dressing up and singing and dancing.'

LYNNE

happily playing with them for hours. Oh, she had her moments – don't get me wrong – she wasn't adverse to the odd tantrum, but she got on with people so well and had such a zest for life. She always had the biggest smile on her face.

'I wanted Louise to read the classics I'd read as a child. But try as I might – and, believe me, I tried – novels like *Little Women* just didn't appeal to her. In fact, nothing interested her as much as music. All she ever wanted to do was put on singing and dancing shows for

She was incredibly popular with all the children and always smiling. We used to call her "the smile on legs".

the family. She'd charge us 25p a ticket to sit in our own front room, which she would strip of furniture to create her "stage". And God help anyone who tried to leave before her final curtain.'

'I was never a natural academic,' sighs Louise, who, despite her obvious loathing of the classroom and her low grades, was a teachers' favourite throughout her school years. 'I was terrible at maths and English. I used to have panic attacks at my first school in Greenwich when I'd have to read things out in class. I was so hopeless at lessons that I ended up with absolutely no confidence in myself.'

It was only Louise's natural ability to entertain and perform that saved her from falling to the bottom of the class in the popularity stakes, a skill which enabled her to make friends and feel involved with the comings and goings of everyday school life. She jumped at every opportunity to appear in school productions and, her mother will tell you, sobbed for days when she failed to clinch the role of Mary in the annual nativity play – only being consoled with the part of "The Christmas Rainbow".

'That was one of my proudest moments,' Louise remembers. 'I had a white leotard with loads of coloured streamers hanging off it that my mum had spent hours sewing on. It was only a small part but I gave it everything I had. I really belted those lines out.'

Having accepted she was not born to a life of academia, Louise contented herself with her small circle of friends in the classroom. But she would race home from school to dive into her dressing-up box as soon as the school bell rang. In the privacy of her bedroom she would escape to the 'Land of Make Believe' – literally, as she mimed for hours to Bucks Fizz records.

'Then, when I was seven, we moved to Eltham, South London. I started at a new school, St Thomas Moore's, and I joined a Saturday

morning class at Della Pointer's dance school. We did ballet, tap, elocu-tion and poetry classes. It was like coming home. I'd found something I was confident and comfortable with. For the first time I felt that I was good at something. My morale was boosted beyond belief. I was still hopeless academically, so bad that I used to pay my friends to do my homework for me. But my life changed dramatically. I discovered that there was (and still is) something about performing that communicates with me and makes me come alive.'

A year after Louise arrived at St Thomas Moore's, the school acknowledged its 50th anniversary with a concert celebrating the five decades. Her headteacher, Eileen Miller, remembers discovering that every class teacher had "pinched" Louise to appear in their performance.

'Our school was big on finding people's talents,' says Mrs Miller. 'And Louise was an incredibly talented performer. But she was also a model pupil. She's right about her written work, it wasn't her strength, but that never stopped her working at it. No matter how hard she struggled with a subject she always gave her best. She was incredibly popular with all the children and always smiling. We used to call her "the smile on legs".'

Each year, Louise would win virtually every singing, dancing and drama competition she entered at the annual Lewisham Dance Festival. It wasn't a surprise to anybody who knew her when she delivered a dazzling performance on Frank Bough's TV show, *Breakfast Time*, after her school won the nationwide competition to compose a song for Prince Andrew and Fergie's wedding. When the time came for her to move to a new school, Mrs Miller decided to intervene. She did not know how influential her input would be on the course of Louise's life.

She telephoned Louise's mum at home. 'The Inner London Education Authority are running scholarships for the Italia Conti Stage School in London. We have an option to enter Louise for the audition, but we have to move quickly, there's only one week left to apply,' Mrs Miller urged, while Lynne Nurding absorbed her suggestion with very little surprise.

'I wasn't too sure about it,' recalls Lynne. 'I mean, Louise was only eleven and she was my little girl. We lived in Eltham and Italia Conti was up in London. I was so worried at the prospect of her travelling by train to school every day, in case something terrible happened to her. I sat down and talked it through with her dad and he said, "We've got to give her the chance." So we did. For the next week, we went to Louise's dance teacher's house after school so she could learn a drama speech, a song and a dance for the audition.'

'My mum and gran came up with me to Italia Conti for the audition because I was so nervous,' remembers Louise. 'The academic entrance exam was awful, I couldn't answer half the questions, but I knew I'd do better in the performance exam. I went into this room with all these other kids and watched for a while as they ran through songs like 'The Good Ship Lollipop' and Andrew Lloyd Webber show tunes. Then I got up there and launched into Gloria Gaynor's 'I Will Survive'. You should have seen the look on the examiners' faces. Their jaws dropped as I launched into 'First I was afraid, I was petrified ...' But I didn't know any different: the only music I knew apart from Bucks Fizz was Tamla Motown, because that's all my dad played round the house. I'd never heard of Andrew Lloyd Webber. I remember leaving the audition and thinking I'd really blown it. But I knew that, whether I got into Italia Conti or not, I wanted to be a performer; for the first time I felt "ambition" burning inside me.'

'I knew that I wanted to be a performer; for the first time I felt "ambition" burning inside me.'

studying for stardom

Amongst the many cards and letters that lay in wait on the Nurdings' doorstep on the morning of 4 November 1985, Louise's eleventh birthday, was one with an East London postmark. As Louise ripped her way through her presents and cards, cannily tipping them open in search of cash, she was stopped in her tracks as her mother began to read out the letter from the East End.

'Guess what, Lou? Here's a lovely birthday present. Italia Conti have accepted you.'

'I was terrified on my first day at Contis,' recalls Louise, who had spent the summer holidays practising the two-hour route to and from school on the train and the tube with her mum. 'Mum came to school with me in the morning, then she'd go home and be back in time to collect me. It meant four hours a day travelling for her. We carried on like that for months, but even having her with me that first day didn't calm me down.'

Sophie, Louise and Kelle practise their dance routines.

The Italia Conti Stage School is well known as a breeding ground for the stars of tomorrow. It's one of Britain's most successful performance academies and has launched the careers of EastEnders' Martine McCutcheon, actress Emily Lloyd and supermodel Naomi Campbell. Emily and Naomi were a year above Louise and she and her friends would watch in wonder, in years to come, as Emily took the lead in school productions in London's West End and gaze in awe as they observed Naomi in dance class.

'But even acknowledging someone like Naomi in the corridor with a nod of the head was implausible to me, on the first day. I just wanted to get through the introductions in assembly,' recalls Louise. 'All the new girls had to gather in Studio 41. I took one look at the dozens of other girls and thought, "What have I done?" I was just about to run out through the door and head for home when I spotted a girl sitting on the floor.'

Louise gravitated in her direction, subconsciously hoping that she would be able to strike up a conversation and a friendship to see her through the day, which loomed ahead. 'It was the first time I'd met

'People think stage schools are an easy bunk-off, but it was incredibly hard work.'

Kelle Bryan,' she remembers, smiling. 'Little did I know back then that we were to become great friends, who would go on to share adventures of every kind in all parts of the world.

'People think that stage schools are an easy bunk-off, but the reality is very different,' says Louise. 'It was incredibly hard work. In the morning we'd do ballet, jazz, tap, singing and acting classes, and after lunch we'd have school work, then at 5 o'clock I'd start the long journey home. I built up great relationships with my teachers, but I was still hopeless at lessons. But sometimes that worked as a blessing in disguise, because I was so bad at biology I got placed next to a girl called Sophie, who to this day is my best friend in the whole world.'

'It was the first time I'd met Kelle Bryan. Little did I know back then that we were to become great friends.'

'We were put together because we were both as bad as each other,' remembers Sophie. 'The teacher said it was like the blind leading the blind – and she wasn't wrong. That was it; as soon as we met we hit it off and became inseparable overnight.'

'Having met Kelle and then Sophie, I knew I was going to be all right at Contis,' says Louise, 'and between the three of us we made some brilliant friends: Letitia, Abby, Charlie and Cathy. To this day we're all still really close.'

The girls networked between one another's homes for weekend sleepovers, and became such regular fixtures within each other's families that their respective mothers knew the dietary preferences of them all. Even now, Louise thinks nothing of popping over to Sophie's when she's out, to sit and have a heart-to-heart with her parents.

'Sophie and I would stay at each other's house all the time. We'd buy sucky sweets, crisps and chocolate and walk around the green, where all the local boys hung out,' says Louise, who rated boys alongside spiders in the 'sexy stakes' until her late teens. 'I had my first kiss in a game of spin-the-bottle, under the slide at the recreation ground, when I was eleven. I didn't kiss anyone again for five years, it seemed like such an unnatural thing to do at the time,' she says, screwing up her face in disgust as she relives her first romantic encounter.

'My cousin told me about sex and I just could not believe it. I thought he was lying to me so I had to go and check it out with my mum. She was a bit embarrassed because I think she thought I was too young to be asking about how babies are made. Boys played such a small part in my life. The whole time I was at Contis I didn't have a boyfriend, or even a date. It sounds pretty sad, but I was completely

Above centre: Dad, brothers, Louise, Sophie,
Letitia and Cathy around the dinner table.
Bottom left: Louise, Mum and little brother Sam at a
friend's wedding, where Louise was a bridesmaid.

dedicated to my work. I had a dream and I wanted to make it come
true. I was reticent when it came to men. If a guy ever did ask me out,
even if I fancied him madly, I was too shy to go. It didn't help that I
looked so young. There were so many beautiful and sophisticated girls
at college. They were all so glamorous, like Naomi Campbell, with legs
as long as a giraffe. And there was me, no more than five foot, looking
about ten years old, with my hair in a ponytail. How on earth could I
compete? I didn't even try.'

'The whole time I was at Contis

I didn't have a boyfriend, or even

a date. It sounds pretty sad, but

I was completely dedicated to my

work. I had a dream and I

wanted to make it come true.'

As the novelty of stage school wore off, Louise and her friends found the confidence to start skiving off lessons. Careful never to leave the site, the girls would find an empty rehearsal studio and while the hours away dreaming up their own dance routines. 'We were always dancing. It was such a big thing in our lives.'

'I was off school for a week with a hangover. One thing for sure,

it put me right off drinking, for good.'

In a cramped living room in the East End of London, Louise and a dozen or so friends danced away at a house party. But that night, Louise's addiction to the dance floor was to lead her into trouble.

'Oh God, not that party!' laughs Louise, when she's reminded of the event. 'I was supposed to be staying with a friend that night on the other side of London, and as soon as I got to the party I started dancing … and I didn't stop. It was really hot and I was getting more and more thirsty, so I kept gulping down pints of blackcurrant that kept appearing at my side. By about 10.30 p.m. I felt so awful I had to lie down on the sofa. My head was spinning and I couldn't open my eyes. No wonder: it turned out to be snakebite I'd been drinking all night.

'All I can remember is someone daring this bloke to eat cat food – and he did. Ugh, I was lying there thinking, "I can't believe he's doing it, I'm going to be sick." I called my mum, told her I thought I had food poisoning, and asked her to come and collect me. I was off school for a week – with a hangover. I've never felt so awful in my life. One thing for sure, it put me right off drinking, for good.'

worries over weight

While Louise may be the babe of the decade according to style bible *Sky* magazine, the curves that would catapult her to beat her fellow student Naomi Campbell in *FHM* magazine's 'The World's 100 Most Beautiful Women' honours list (Louise came second, Naomi 93rd) were the bane of her life as a teenager.

Alongside Charlie, Sophie and Kelle, Louise became obsessed with her weight and her diet before the end of her first year at Italia Conti and, surrounded by ballerinas and supermodels of the future, she embarked upon years of extreme dieting. Her eating habits stopped short of anorexia only because the shock of seeing other girls at school come close to starvation snapped her out of it.

'I went through that puppy-fat stage when I was at Italia Conti. At fourteen I started getting boobs and a bum and my face filled out. For a dancer, that's a death knell. I'd go to auditions for commercials – which I never got – and find the room would be filled with skinny, under-developed girls with perfect skin,' sighs Louise, who now wears a healthy size-10 dress. 'Who wouldn't feel inferior in an environment like that? We all struggled with our weight: Kelle, Sophie, Charlie and me.

'For years, Charlie and I would share a buttered roll for lunch every day. That's all we'd have. And when Sophie stayed at my house we'd get a Chinese takeaway, have two mouthfuls and throw the rest away out of guilt.' One by one the girls fell, like flies, into disturbed eating habits. (Eating disorders aren't by any means exclusive to stage schools: one in four girls suffers with anorexia or bulimia these days.) Meal times, and avoiding them, became all that Louise and her friends thought about.

Lynne Nurding was concerned, as any mother would be, and was more aware of Louise's aversion to eating than her daughter gave her credit for. 'Dieting was a major worry for us when Louise was at Italia Conti,' remembers Lynne. 'I think the obsession comes from standing in front of mirrors at school all day long.

'It was a tough life for the girls: always auditioning and dealing with constant let downs. Lou did get a couple of adverts and a panto,

'Life is too

important to

spend all your

time worrying

about what

you look like.'

though. She played the cat in *Dick Whittington* with *Rainbow's* Rod, Jane and Freddy, at a theatre in Wimbledon. Every night when she came home, she'd tell me she'd already eaten, when I was sure she hadn't.

'She was always sneaking in the fridge when she thought nobody was watching, just picking little bits: a bit broken off the crust of a pie or a spoonful of yoghurt out of the tub. It was painfully obvious that she was almost starving herself. Although she still won't eat any more than she has to, Louise now realises that she has to eat a certain amount to survive and be healthy. I'd like her to eat more, but as the old saying goes: you can lead a horse to water (or a plate of food) but you can't make it drink … or eat.'

'I thought I was being so clever at the time, but looking back I realise my mum must have known something was going on,' says Louise. 'I started drawing up ridiculous diets for myself. In effect, I virtually stopped eating because I didn't know how else to lose weight. Sometimes I'd go days without food. I'd be so tired from what I thought was dancing at school all day; now I realise that lack of food leaves you exhausted and utterly miserable. Of course my mum was desperately worried about me. I used to lie to her about what I'd eaten at school so I could get out of my evening meal. People thought I was on the verge of anorexia, but I wasn't. I was lucky I snapped out of it when I did.'

Sensible eating was something Louise would learn later: when Sophie was hospitalised because of her anorexia at the age of sixteen, when she was working as a fashion model.

'I was well on the way to anorexia when I left Italia Conti,' explains Sophie, who now shares a house with Louise in London and works as a dancer. 'The illness took over my life. I was very depressed and very ill and ended up in hospital. But throughout it all, Louise never stopped being a friend. Sometimes I was horrible to her because I wasn't myself, but she was so understanding and supportive. All the girls were.'

'I still don't have the best body-image in the world. I like my hands, but I don't like my legs because they're not long enough and I've got knees like a footballer. But I've come to realise that life's too important to spend all your time worrying about what you look like,' concludes Louise. 'You only get one shot at life, so you have to make the most of it. But even now I have to watch what I eat. When I'm performing I want to look the best I can. I don't have a model's figure and I'm never going to be six foot, so I work out to get fit. Today I'm sensible with my diet to the extent where I feel happy with my weight. And it's not for anybody else – it's for me.'

ple thought I

on the verge

norexia ,

I wasn't.'

clubbing and fun

'**I** really got into clubbing with the girls when I was fourteen. Even though we were under age, we used to go to clubs in London and we'd dance all night. We loved SW1 in Victoria and The Milk Bar in Soho, but it was always a problem getting past the doormen because I looked so young – about twelve on a good day!' giggles Louise, as she revisits her early clubbing experiences. 'Standing in a queue, trembling with fear in case you get turned away, is something every teenager lives through – but I lived it well into my twenties. Even now I get asked for ID.'

It's a scenario most of us have gone through at one time in our lives. Louise would hide amongst her older-looking friends as they tottered their way into London's trendiest nightclubs in platform shoes. 'Every time we went out we'd put Cathy at the front of the queue because she looked so much older and everyone fancied her,' remembers Louise, laughing. 'She's just naturally gorgeous. In ballet class at school, our studio was directly facing a building site, Cathy would make after-school dates with the builders as she stretched out over the exercise bar.

'When we went out I'd hide behind her with my head down. I looked so under age and completely unsexy. It's amazing that we ever got in anywhere, but we did – every time. Even when I was inside I'd be so paranoid I'd spend all night on the dance floor in my Gary Glitter platforms in the hope that nobody would catch me out. I wasn't interested in drinking and I most certainly wasn't into men. In fact, I was never the remotest bit interested in going out with men, probably because I never attracted them in hordes like my friends did. Blokes just weren't interested in me. I think, because I couldn't pull, I decided I didn't like them.

'The night I met Denis in The Milk Bar must have been fate. When he came over and talked to me and told me to call him, I didn't think he was a creep on the pull or a bloke out on the blag, I knew he was for real. I was excited by what he had to say but I didn't take it too

'I was never

the remotest

bit interested

in going out

with men.'

seriously. Although, I must admit, I couldn't wait to get home and tell Mum and Dad. Kelle's dad picked us up from the club that night – all our parents took it in turns to drive us, they were good like that – and as he drove us home I kept thinking about how I was going to tell my mum about Denis. I couldn't say I had met him in a club: it was a school night and I'd told her I was staying in round at Kelle's house.'

THE NURDING HOME, ELTHAM. THE NEXT DAY

Louise tries to disguise her excitement when she shows her parents Denis Ingoldsby's card.

LOUISE: Mum, Dad, you'll never believe what's happened. A manager gave me his card and asked me to call him.

DAD: Well, you can throw that straight in the bin, Lou. Don't forget you're only fifteen.

MUM: Oh Lou, you can't go accepting cards from strange men. Good heavens knows what he wants. Do as your dad says and forget about it.

LOUISE: But Mum, you can't say no, this could be my big chance. Pleeease!!! I've got to give it a go. You know you can trust me.

DAD: That card belongs in the bin – and don't think about fishing it out.

LOUISE: I can't believe this. You're ruining my life.

Fortunately, Louise had made a copy of Denis's number on the back of her school bus-pass, but six months passed before she plucked up the courage to use it – without her parents knowing. She finally made contact with Denis shortly before her sixteenth birthday.

'It was more than six months before I heard from Louise,' recalls Denis Ingoldsby. 'When she told me she was only fifteen and that I'd need to speak to her mum and dad to convince them I wasn't weird, I could've passed out on the spot. Fifteen! I just couldn't believe it.

'The moment I set eyes on Louise, I knew there was something special about her. And she didn't seem to be aware of just how magnetic she was. I'm glad she was there that night, because I was right when I said she could be the next Madonna. There's something people love about Lou, her innocence I think. She's very real, very warm and ... well, she's good-looking, isn't she?'

Lynne Nurding remembers this time well. 'After we'd told Louise the big NO, not much was spoken about Denis for a couple of months. But it was obvious that Louise wasn't going to give up on it. She can be very determined, you know. Unbeknown to me, Louise had been in touch with him and had asked him to call me and Tim to explain that he was what he said he was. Denis told us that he understood what we were thinking, but that he'd like us to come up and meet him so he could put a proposal to us. Louise persuaded us to go and meet him, and his partner Oliver, at a rehearsal studio.'

At the MCA Studios in Hammersmith, Oliver Smallman (the business super-brain behind 1st Avenue Records) and Denis (the man

'There's

something

people love

about Lou,

her

innocence

I think...'

DENIS

with a Midas touch in the studio) were overseeing the final mix of Dina Carroll's debut album (which went on to be the biggest selling debut album of the year).

Tim, Lynne and Louise arrived at 7 p.m. and the two men took them to the office to discuss their plans for developing Louise's career. While the adults talked, Denis let Louise loose in the recording studio for the first time, giving her a taste of life as a pop star.

An hour later, Louise and her parents headed home to Eltham, happily assured that Louise – and her career – would be more than safe in the hands of 1st Avenue.

eternal
are born

Louise wandered around the MCA Studios in Hammersmith, looking for Denis. It was only the second time she'd been in a professional recording studio and she got a buzz from spotting famous faces – people whose records she loved to dance, and sometimes sing along, to. 'I was so impressed with what I saw and heard down there,' she remembers, with a smile. 'Even though there were loads of famous people there, everyone was really friendly and unstarry. Boy George came over and said "Hi" and I was so surprised that he'd take any notice of me that it was all I could do to stop myself from singing "Karma, karma, karma, karma, karma chameleon". I kept thinking to myself, "Keep cool, Lou, keep cool." I blurted out hello and rushed off to find Denis, just so I could tell him I'd met Boy George.'

When Lou finally tracked Denis down – he's not the easiest of people to keep tabs on – he took her into a recording studio where two girls were laying backing vocals. 'Louise,' said Denis, with a flash of his trademark Cheshire Cat grin, 'meet Easther and Vernie Bennett.'

All three girls smiled at each other and set about exchanging idle gossip for the rest of the day. What the girls didn't realise at the time was that Denis had engineered the meeting with a mind to putting them together in a group. But nobody – not even Denis – had an inkling that within two years they would become the most successful girl group in Britain.

LOUISE ON EASTHER: She had the best voice I'd ever heard. But she wasn't full of herself. I hit it off with Easther straight away, we really clicked. We liked the same music and, coincidentally, we were both wearing exactly the same boots. You could be girlie with her, she was fun. We swapped numbers and promised to get in touch.

LOUISE ON VERNIE: She seemed so much older and more mature than me. From day one, she was like the mother of the group. I could tell from the moment I met her that she was really together and sorted. Everything about Vernie is sorted, she's very bright and on the ball. I knew just from talking to both Vernie and Easther that we were different people from different backgrounds, but that wasn't a problem. From the start I knew they were very religious and that

'Boy George came over and said "Hi" and I was so surprised that he'd take any notice of me.'

wasn't an issue with me because the Church, and God, is a very important part of my family's life.

Denis Ingoldsby had a vision a long time before he met Louise, Easther and Vernie. He wanted to create Britain's answer to En Vogue. His inspired concept came to life the day he spotted Vernie singing at a talent night held at a London club called Xenon. He gave her his number, but she never called him back. Determined to secure her talents in his latest project, Denis went down to Xenon the following week to try and persuade her to sign up. Instead of talking Vernie around, he became sidetracked by another, equally impressive, female singer. She

turned out to be far more responsive than Vernie and snatched a card out of his hand almost before he could even offer it. What he didn't realise was that he'd met Vernie's kid sister: Easther Bennett. And true to style, Easther wasted no time in meeting Denis, dragging Vernie along into the bargain, much to Denis's surprise.

Mrs Bennett is a pastor and started the girls off singing in her Croydon church choir when they were toddlers. Needless to say, she wasn't impressed when Vernie arrived home from her meeting with Denis to announce she was going to have to drop out of her Law and Philosophy degree course at Wolverhampton University if, and when, the pop group she and Easther had just joined took off.

One month after Louise met Easther and Vernie, Denis called her at home to make sure she'd kept her word and stayed in contact with them. He'd been waiting for the girls to strike up a natural friendship before putting them together officially as a group. Now he felt the time was right to put the wheels into motion. All that was left to do was to find another member for the group to make it up to a four piece, and then he could start rehearsing them.

DENIS: Listen, have you called the girls yet?

LOUISE: Sorry, I've been busy with school. I will call them though. How are they?

DENIS: On top form, so why don't I fix something up? I'll organise a studio on Monday and you can all get together. Oh, and by the way, another girl I had in mind to work with the three of you has dropped out. Do you know anyone who can sing and dance?

LOUISE: Yeah. I know just the girl. You'll love her. See you on Monday.

As soon as Louise hung up from Denis she dialled Kelle's number.

whitney houston calls

'**D**on't be nervous, Kelle, it'll be cool,' said Louise soothingly, when the two girls arrived at the MCA Studios to meet up with Easther and Vernie.

And Lou was right, Kelle hit it off with Easther and Vernie like a house on fire.

Two hours later, back at Kelle's house – where the two girls spent many nights watching Freddy Kruger videos and pigging out on tea, toast and Crunchy Nut Cornflakes – Louise asked Kelle what she thought of the Bennett sisters.

'Yeah. They're all right, aren't they?' said Kelle, hiding her face behind a pillow.

'That was all she said,' remembers Lou. 'She was more worried about the nightmares she knew she'd be having later. We spent many nights scaring ourselves watching horror films and then sleeping together in the living room with a cross under our pillows. I can't believe we used to do that. We were sixteen at the time which, looking back, makes us seriously sad.'

Oliver Smallman fondly recalls meeting Louise for the first time, just two days after all four girls had finally met each other, when Denis was putting them through their paces in a rehearsal studio at the Dance Attic in Putney, south-west London. It was very early days, so they still looked like complete strangers to me,' remembers Oliver, who is famed – and sometimes feared – for his razor-sharp business sense. 'I thought there were clearly two brilliant dancers in Louise and Kelle, that one of the sisters had a fantastic voice, but that nobody in particular stood out. However, I did notice that Louise conducted herself incredibly well. She was impossible to dislike,' he adds.

Denis, who admits to being a hard taskmaster when the occasion calls, spent the next two years developing the girls. With Louise and Kelle still at Contis, Easther working in MacDonalds, and Vernie still struggling to keep up with her Law degree in between trips to London for band meetings, it was difficult to find time for the girls to rehearse. But they were all more than happy to give up every evening and weekend to master their craft.

'Dancing was the only thing I'd ever been good at and sometimes I felt so discouraged. But I stuck at it.'

' We practised really hard to get it

all together, spending every spare

hour after school and most weekends

in the studio, recording tracks and

getting our routines tight. '

'We practised really hard to get it all together, spending every spare hour after school and most weekends in the studio, recording tracks and getting our routines tight. We had a choreographer who gave me a hard time, always shouting at me,' remembers Louise, thinking of the nights when money was so tight that the girls would practise in the cheapest dance studio they could find, with rain dripping through holes in the ceiling, and the worry about having enough cash for the bus fare home. 'Denis would make sure that we did everything again and again and again until it was perfect,' says Lou. 'That was hard. Dancing was the only thing I'd ever been good at and sometimes I felt so discouraged. But I stuck at it.'

The girls' devotion to rehearsals paid off. Not only were they a pop group, they sang and danced like a pop group too. All that was needed now was a 'look'. Louise remembers how, for a sixteen-year-old who had never even plucked her eyebrows, creating a stage image didn't come naturally.

'I was always so unprepared for anything outside the actual performance,' she says. 'I was so nervous about doing the showcase, when we were trying for a record deal. I wasn't nervous about the performance, but because I had to go out and buy an outfit and I didn't have a clue what to wear. In the end we got a deal with EMI after we sang a cappella to them over at the park close to the offices, wearing jeans, T-shirts and big, chunky boots. Sophisticated, eh?'

On the night of Eternal's showcase, where they were to perform to a critical audience made up of record company executives, Louise was battling with her nerves backstage when a faintly familiar face was shown into the girls' dressing room. 'There was this woman standing there wishing us luck. Suddenly it dawned on me who it was and all I could say when she said she was pleased to meet me was "Oh my God, it's Brooke Shields",' says Louise, cringing. 'I was so nervous that the rest of the night passed in a haze. I still can't remember much about it.'

Despite Eternal's instant recognition and acclaim, Louise kept her feet firmly on the ground and her ego in check. Her ability to do that reveals qualities that those who know her still admire in her today. 'Nobody knew at Contis, except for her closest friends, that Louise was in a group,' recalls Charlie. 'One day, at school, she played me a fantastic tape of a song called "Stay". I couldn't believe it when she said, "It's me. It's the group I'm in. It's going to be our first single, but please don't tell anyone." It was the best thing I'd heard for years and it sent a tingle up my spine.'

Life took off like a roller coaster for the girls. Eternal was a buzz word in the music industry and, before they'd even released a record, they were supporting Dina Carroll on tour and playing at Radio 1 Roadshows around England. For Louise, it was a hard decision to take

'Whitney

wished us

ıck and said

God bless.

/e were like:

"Wow!

Whitney

Houston".'

the plunge and leave Italia Conti, and her friends, to concentrate on her career with Eternal.

But within a week of leaving Italia Conti, she was on a plane flying to New York to shoot the video for Eternal's debut single, 'Stay'. It was a thrill for all the girls, but Louise says it was the experience in a Nashville recording studio that would become the highlight of the year.

Eternal were working in a studio with the legendary producer and songwriter cousin of Whitney Houston, BeBe Winans – who would later go on to give Eternal their first number one when he sang with them on 'I Wanna Be The Only One' – when the phone went. Louise recalls: 'It was Whitney Houston! We were speechless because we all adored Whitney. She said she hoped everything went well for us, wished us luck and said God bless. It was amazing. We were like: "Wow! Whitney Houston".'

eternal
are a hit

'The early days in the group were so much fun,' remembers Louise, of the year when Eternal's unprecedented chart success turned them into the hottest new group in the charts. 'Every day was like a new adventure, but the highlight had to be doing the *Smash Hits* tour with all the young groups, like Boyzone, Worlds Apart and Peter Andre. We got such a brilliant reaction from the fans, even though most of them were only really there to scream their heads off at the boys. I think the girls in the audience could relate to us, and our music, because we weren't all tarted up in short skirts and caked with make-up. The fans knew we weren't there to pull the boys from the bands. I think anyone who saw us on that tour could see we were just happy to have a go on stage every night.'

While the fans loved Eternal's image, the boys on the *Smash Hits* tour were astonished by their lack of glamour and vanity. 'We used to turn up at gigs in what we were going to wear on stage, you know: jeans, big shirts, boots, and no make-up,' says Louise, smiling at the memory of her early 'image' as an eighteen-year-old. 'I remember, one day, Worlds Apart were in their dressing room getting changed and they took one look at us and said, "Aren't you going to get changed, you're on in a minute?" We said, "Cheek! We're going on like this." They just stood there, changing into their matching silky shirts, with their mouths open in surprise.'

While Eternal were building up a formidable fan base around the country, their debut single, 'Stay', was released in October 1993. To the girls' astonishment, it went straight into the charts at number four. It was followed a month later by 'Always and Forever', which went on to become the biggest selling debut album of the year, with a colossal 1.5 million sales.

With typical modesty, Louise recounts hearing the news that Eternal had 'done it'. 'We were working, doing a radio show, when Denis called to say we'd charted ... at number four. I was so thrilled. But I didn't want to look flash and, thinking about it, I don't think it really sank in – everything was happening so fast – so I only really celebrated when I got home and was alone in my bedroom.'

'The early days in the group were so much fun, every day was like a new adventure.'

Top of the Pops was the obvious next port of call for Eternal. It was only just before the girls headed off to the BBC studio in Shepherd's Bush that Louise finally admitted to herself that Eternal was no longer something she could keep secret from her school friends. After all, they were stage school students, *Tops of the Pops* was compulsory viewing.

'There was such a buzz going round Contis when Eternal first released "Stay", everyone was playing it and making up dance routines,' recalls Charlie, proudly. 'It was brilliant watching Lou for the first time on *Top of the Pops*. As soon as her bit was over, all her old friends called one another up, screaming at each other down the phone with excitement because we were so proud of her. Even today, I get a tingle down my spine whenever I see her perform.'

'It was really quite exciting,' says Tim Nurding, recalling Louise's début on *Top of the Pops*. 'The family sat down together to watch and we were so proud. So many kids could have got bigheaded after being on telly, but Louise came home that night the same girl she'd always been. Even today, with all the success she's had, she hasn't changed a bit.'

Louise's down-to-earth personality was to stand her in good stead as Eternal rapidly shot to fame around the world. The following months proved to be a heady and exhausting whirl of touring, television appearances, interviews, video and photographic shoots, as the girls travelled the globe, promoting 'Always and Forever' and the ever-increasing collection of top ten singles.

'We were all over the world, working hard and feeling absolutely shattered,' says Louise, of the early days when Eternal were securing their international star status. 'We were having top tens all over the place, and that was when it hit me for the first time that we were really doing well. It was such a strange experience. I can completely understand why some people become self-indulgent when they become successful, because you have people running around after your every whim.'

However, their new-found fame came with a price. Even though the girls were exhausted from such a punishing schedule, they sacrificed rare holidays to further Eternal's success abroad. The girls reluctantly abandoned their plans to see in the New Year with friends and family in London, to perform at a gig in Germany on New Year's Eve 1993. The trip was a disaster. Not only did they have to cope with dodging a series of stray fireworks that exploded on stage, but Vernie and Kelle were struck down with chronic food poisoning. They were so determined not to let down their fans by cancelling the gig that they carried on, rushing off stage during numbers to throw up in a bucket in the wings.

Later that night, after Kelle and Vernie had collapsed in their hotel beds, Louise and Easther tried to salvage what was left of the

'I was so

nervous

about doing

the show-

case, when

we were

trying for a

record deal.'

New Year celebrations at a local nightclub. 'It was an absolute nightmare,' remembers Louise. 'We saw in 1994 in the worst club I've been to in my life. They played the theme track from *The Rocky Horror Show* all night. For two days after that I couldn't get the lyrics "Let's do the time warp again ..." out of my mind. That was the first, and last, time we ever worked on New Year's Eve.'

Away from her family and friends, and busy coping within an alien and high-pressured environment, Louise kept in touch with her home life with regular phone calls. Denis kept true to his promise to Louise's parents that he would look after their little girl.

'In the early days, Denis always phoned me to let me know she was fine. He'd phone from America, Europe, wherever they were. But I don't think he had a clock,' laughs Lynne Nurding. 'He'd phone at all times of the day and night.'

With their new-found success, the girls inevitably started attracting attention from fans of the opposite sex. 'We never really got hassled by men. To be honest, most of them would politely ask for an autograph, say they liked the music and then run off. We weren't exactly glamorous sex-kittens,' laughs Louise, whose features have since adorned thousands of bedroom, and office, walls. 'But there were some weird men who'd send us videos of themselves, talking as if we were close friends, for the entire length of a three-hour tape. Others would turn up in the front row of every gig, whether it was in America, Australia or Europe. One bloke who followed us around the world called me in my hotel room when I was in Thailand and said, "Hi, it's me. I'm in town." It was incredibly flattering that he wanted to follow our career, but I used to wonder where he got the money from to do all that travelling.'

One of the worst experiences she suffered at the hands of an over-enthusiastic fan was when, during Eternal's first British tour, they were in the middle of singing 'Oh Baby' (which had gone straight in the charts at number four on Bonfire Night, the day after Louise's twentieth birthday). Louise spotted a man in the front row, acting strangely. 'He was being really, really disgusting,' she says, still somewhat shocked by the memory. 'That was the end of my harmonies, I can tell you.'

With the exception of the occasional 'odd-bod', Eternal's fans were a constant source of happiness – and, eventually, reassurance – for Louise, as were the group's remarkable accomplishments in the international charts. 'In such a short time we'd achieved everything we'd ever wanted. It was like a dream come true. But the best times for me were when we were playing live to an audience. I'd look down from the stage and they'd know every word and you could stop singing and they'd sing back to you. My eyes would well up and I'd think, "Oh my God, there's just nothing like it".'

'I'd look down from the stage and they'd know every word and you could stop singing and they'd sing back to you.'

I want to go home

Suddenly the hairbrush had become a microphone, the mirror a real, live audience and Bucks Fizz a distant – and sometimes embarrassing – memory of Louise's childhood ambitions. She was the singer she'd always dreamt of being. She should have been the happiest girl in the world. Eternal were riding high, 'Always and Forever' had made it into the record books, the girls were earning more money than they'd ever dreamt of, and were travelling around the world first class to places they often never even knew existed and mixing with the glitterati.

But despite their phenomenal success, Louise was desperately unhappy, and had been for a long time. She felt isolated, confused, alone, and downright depressed. The more miserable she became, the more she withdrew from the group, which only added to the distance that was growing between her and the girls. She spent nights alone in her hotel room in foreign lands trying to figure out why she felt so low. The sun would often rise before she gave up searching for an answer and finally drifted into an unsettled sleep.

For eighteen months she lived with her increasing unhappiness, but eventually had to face up to the fact that the time had come to think long and hard about her future. Yet, the prospect of leaving Eternal and venturing into the unknown was never going to be an easy decision to make. 'A part of me was the happiest person in the world, but the other part had had enough. I just wanted to go home. I'd reached the stage where success wasn't enough any more,' says Louise, sadly describing how life in Eternal wasn't panning out as she had hoped.

'It took eighteen months to pluck up the courage to admit to myself that I wanted out. I felt trapped and knew in my heart it wasn't right for me. I'd got to the stage where I felt so uncomfortable that if I didn't get out it would seriously affect my health.'

Louise's unhappiness began to affect every waking, and sleeping, moment of her life to such a degree that she plummeted into an anxious depression. 'When I was in the group, I used to have nightmares and then wake up every morning with a knot of nervousness in

'I felt trapped and knew in my heart it wasn't right for me.'

my stomach,' she says. 'I'd be worrying about what the day would bring, but would know that I had absolutely no control over what I'd end up doing. I felt so isolated, so on my own, that I couldn't talk to anyone else. I got to the stage where I couldn't even eat. The girls got mad at me because they thought I had an eating disorder. But the reason I wasn't eating was because I was so unhappy I didn't want to enjoy anything or give myself any pleasure. I didn't want to eat an ice cream because it tasted nice and I didn't want to feel nice any more. I was caught in a rut of feeling down and the only way to break it was to break out.

'I didn't want to tell the others I wasn't enjoying being in the group. Let's face it, it was meant to be the best time of our lives, they didn't need me putting a downer on everything. So I just kept everything I was feeling to myself. But I was crying down the phone to my mum most nights.'

Understandably, Lynne Nurding was desperately concerned as she watched her once-happy daughter with the ever-bright smile transform into an unconfident and tearful shadow of her former happy-go-lucky self. 'I just wanted Lou to be happy,' says Lynne. 'But it was getting worse as time wore on. It broke our hearts trying to keep up a brave face for Louise. There'd be those awful late-night phone calls from all over the world when she was so sad, but we couldn't do anything to help her except listen, try to understand and just be there all the time for her.'

Sophie and Charlie watched helplessly. 'She lost her sparkle. All her confidence went, she lost so much weight and we never saw her smile any more,' says Charlie. 'I was working in Greece at the time but I knew just from speaking to Lou that she was low. I'd never heard her like that before. It worried me.'

While her family and friends were concerned about her, Louise battled to understand the root of her problems within Eternal. 'We didn't hate each other, in fact I love them all dearly and I would never hear a bad word against any of the girls. It's just that, as people, we were wrong together. We were from different worlds and we had such different views on everything,' she says, sadly. 'The little things started to become issues. I wanted to wear a skirt on stage and that was against group policy. There were rules and regulations about not having people backstage which I found hard at times because I couldn't share what I was doing with people I loved. Eternal was supposed to become "the family". I totally understand that having people backstage all the time would have been hard for the others, but sometimes I felt like I needed people there.

'It just wasn't running smoothly anymore. It was a total communication breakdown.'

'And the girls used to get so mad at me because I lost so much confidence in myself,' Louise continues. 'I became very laid back and didn't put anything into the group when it came to making decisions, which must have been frustrating for the others. I think they thought I didn't care. But what the girls didn't realise was that I lost more and more confidence the more I struggled to communicate with them. It became a vicious circle. It wasn't that anybody was being particularly nasty to anyone, it just wasn't running smoothly anymore. It was a total communication breakdown.

'It got to the stage where even Kelle wasn't there any more as just a friend. Working with her meant things had sort of changed and, while I withdrew, she found a friendship with Easther and Vernie. At the time, I wanted to blame someone for me wanting to leave Eternal. I thought maybe it was because they were horrible to me. But when I look back now I understand that it works both ways. It must have been very hard for them coping with me being so unhappy.

'Part of me really wanted to stay because I loved everything about the style and the music of the group. But I just didn't feel I fitted in well enough, not even with Kelle at this point. Even though she's one of my best friends, I didn't feel on a level where I could work with them anymore.'

Louise finally made the decision to leave when she was alone one night in another faceless hotel room, in a country she can't even remember. 'As much as I loved the girls, in the end I had to make the break because my health, as well as my state of mind, was suffering.

'I remember every detail of that night. It was so scary, but at the same time very liberating. I was sitting in my hotel room alone and the girls were eating together in another room. I realised that we'd lost the connection between us: I'd shut them out and they'd shut me out. I knew I had to go. I called my mum and said, "I'm leaving." I flew home the next day and phoned Denis and Oliver to explain. And that was it. The end. It was the hardest – and saddest – thing I've ever had to do.'

'It had been brewing for months,' recalls Denis, who had become a good friend as well as a good manager to Louise. 'She would cry to me nearly every night because she wasn't happy. It was on my birthday when she told me that she wanted to leave. It was very hard for me because I'd put the group together. I feel very paternal towards all of them. It was really sad, for everyone involved, but I told Lou she had my support in whatever she wanted to do. I knew it would have happened one day, but I just wasn't expecting it after the first album. Telling me certainly wasn't an easy thing for Lou to do, but telling the girls … Even I cried.'

'Part of me really wanted to stay because I loved everything about the style and the music of the group.'

louise calls it a day

'I felt physically sick with nerves on that drive to 1st Avenue's offices to tell the girls I was leaving,' remembers Louise with a shudder. 'After everything we'd been through together it was such a hard thing to explain, especially because I couldn't really explain to myself why I had to leave, let alone to anyone else. I took a deep breath and tried not to show how scared I was, but my legs were shaking like jelly.'

Inside the building that had, over the past four years, become like a second home to the twenty-year-old, a place where she had shared the highs and lows of Eternal's success, Oliver and Denis were waiting to start the meeting. They hugged Louise before she went in, to show their support. Kelle, Easther and Vernie were sitting round the table chatting and laughing without an inkling as to what was to come, when Oliver announced, 'Lou's got something to tell you.'

'My mind was racing. As much as there were times when we didn't get on and as much as we were different, I felt such a strong love for them then, I felt really close to them,' says Louise. 'I just said, "I'm leaving the group." They all looked so shocked. Vernie asked me why and I tried to explain how I felt. We had a long, long talk about why I was unhappy and everything that had happened between us over the past eighteen months fell into place. Kelle had sensed I was unhappy and she knew nothing would change my mind, so she didn't even try to talk me round. The worst of it all was when I looked at Easther's face and she had tears in her eyes: it made me cry too. We were both sitting there sobbing and she kept saying, "You don't have to do this. We can work it out." But I knew in my heart that I did have to do it.'

Louise knew that she needed a new musical direction, that she wanted to do pop and, most importantly, that she wanted her freedom. It was Oliver and Denis who came to the rescue with a solution to all their problems: getting Louise a solo deal.

'It was definitely the biggest shock I've had in the record business. If a group split up because they're not doing very well it's something you can relate to,' says Oliver. 'Louise's timing was surprising.

'After everything

we'd been

through together

it was such a

hard thing to

explain.'

'My mind was racing. As much as
there were times when we didn't get
on and as much as we were different,
I felt such a strong love for them.'

It was a huge gamble on her part. Let's face it, not many people give up a group that's sold two million albums, and is the biggest girl group in the country, to pursue a solo career. Luckily, we had a very cooperative managing director at EMI Records who gave us his full support to start Lou's solo career.'

    Oliver and Denis took the bull by the horns, and before Louise went home that night she was the proud owner of a solo recording contract with EMI. Having promised that she would finish the promotion for Eternal's debut album, and would give Denis and Oliver six months to lay foundations for her solo outing before the news was released to the world, Louise went home to contemplate her future.

    'After I told the girls, I felt total relief. I was scared, but I felt so good for the first time in a long time,' says Louise. 'I knew I wanted to do pop, but I didn't know how I'd realise that goal, or even if it would work out. It was the biggest decision I'd ever had to make in my whole life. I was terrified, so scared. But I had grown and needed to start a new chapter in my life.'

    Louise's imminent departure was the best-kept secret in the music business. While nobody outside of the Eternal circle had any idea that things were amiss, the girls were struggling to readjust to the new situation.

    For the next month, Easther called Louise every day to make sure she was OK. 'I was having nightmares all the time and was worried about whether or not I'd made the right decision. It was so good to know that the girls were still there for me and still cared,' says Louise. 'Easther would call me up every day and say, "Lou, are you sure you want to do this? If there's any problems let's talk them over, don't just leave us without trying to sort it out." I'll always love her for that, she has a good heart, Easther. But when she realised my mind was made up, she told me I could always go back to Eternal. But I knew that I never would.'

    Louise's last day with Eternal, on 23 June 1995, was an emotional one. The girls had gone to the Silver Clef Awards in London to pick up an award. As Louise sat in the audience, waiting for the moment when they would be called to the stage, the reality that soon she would no longer be part of Eternal really hit home.

    'It was so sad,' says Louise. 'We all had to go up and get an award, and everyone close to us knew I was leaving. I remember Easther holding my hand as we stood in front of the audience and I was thinking: I can't do it, I can't leave. But something inside me had made that decision. And I had to see it through.'

'After I told
the girls, I felt
total relief. I
was scared,
but I felt so
good for the
first time in a
long time.'

going solo: a new beginning

In the three months following her departure from Eternal, Louise shut herself off from the world and stayed at home with her parents as she struggled to come to terms with her new-found status. She was so confused that she distanced herself from the music industry to the degree where she was unable to listen to music; even on long car journeys she would insist upon silence.

'Every song was a reminder of what I'd given up, or was by someone I knew, and the only thing I was certain of in my life at that time was that I wanted to be a singer so much it hurt. But, to be honest, I didn't know if I'd ever get the chance to go into a recording studio again or hear one of my songs on the radio. Listening to other people doing what I wanted to do – and had been doing only a few weeks earlier – was torture. It was worse than being on a diet and working in a cake shop.'

As well as cutting out music from her life, she also stopped reading newspapers, magazines and any form of literature which was related to music and celebrities. This meant that Louise was blissfully unaware she was being quickly singled out in the music press and men's glossy magazines as the most popular female in the pop world. Rarely would you read an interview with a boy band or footballer without them citing her as their "ultimate babe". Louise was an 'It' girl before the genre was even invented.

But she attracted a curious mix of fans. It wasn't just the boys who loved her, the women fell for her too. They knew Louise was a mate rather than a man-eater, that she wasn't out to steal their boyfriends and that she was the sort of girl who was reliable in a crisis (always on standby with a box of Kleenex and the offer of a cup of tea and a heart-to-heart).

In hindsight, it seems an obvious move for Louise to utilise her talents and individuality by embarking upon a solo career. But when the news was released of her departure from Eternal, it came as a shock to her fans and friends, few of whom she had told. But fate dealt Louise a lucky hand. One day after the announcement was made of her departure into solo waters, the story broke that Robbie Williams

'The only thing I was certain of in my life at that time was that I wanted to be a singer so much it hurt.'

had left Take That. For Louise, it was a blessing in disguise. It took the heat off, allowing her the privacy to start the new chapter in her life without the added strain of media attention.

Inevitably, rumours of what had prompted Louise to leave Eternal were becoming more far-fetched by the hour. People were speculating as to whether she'd been kicked out, or been a victim of racial tension within the group, others suggested that she had simply got too big for her boots, while some believed that she and Robbie Williams were planning to release a duet together. The stories ranged from the sublime to the ridiculous. But throughout all this, says Louise, it was the support of the fans which gave her the strength to carry on.

'I had been really worried that nobody would ever want to buy my records and that the fans would hate me for leaving, but I got some great letters saying "We're really sad you're leaving, reconsider for us, please!", while others just said "Congratulations!", or "You have to follow your heart". I was so touched.'

Meanwhile, Denis and Oliver had shot into overdrive to launch Louise's solo career. The decision about what would be her first release as a solo artist was, obviously, crucial. Simon Climie, the former pop star turned award-winning songwriter and producer – whose hits include George Michael and Aretha Franklin's 'Knew You Were Waiting For Me' – had recently joined 1st Avenue and was playing a new ballad he'd written, called 'Light of my Life', to Oliver and Denis.

'They said the song would be fantastic for an artist of theirs, but at first they wouldn't tell me who it was,' recalls Simon. 'They asked me if I could do it

by the following Thursday. On the Thursday they sat me down and said, "This is so top secret that if you tell anyone we'll kill you." And I'm sure they meant it,' Simon remembers, laughing. 'They told me Louise was leaving Eternal and that the song I'd written was going to be her début solo single. Then they brought Louise in and made me sing the song to her. They were all watching me and I was so embarrassed. But Louise was lovely, so down to earth. She listened and said, "I love that song. Can I do it?"'

Meanwhile, the recording studio was booked so they could start at 10 a.m. the following morning.

Her first day in the studio as a solo artist was a milestone for Louise to overcome. Although she was excited beyond belief, for the first time in her professional career she had only herself to rely upon. It was, quite literally, make or break time – and Louise was well aware of it.

Simon remembers the anxieties Louise went through, as she crafted her first single. 'We all believed in Louise, but I'm not so sure she had complete confidence in herself at the beginning. Being in a group where the singing was shared meant that Louise had never sung a whole song all the way through by herself. She was obviously a little shy and nervous, but we all knew she had star quality, there's something magical about her. And within two minutes of her opening her mouth I knew she had a great voice.'

But it wasn't just Louise's talent as an artist that had attracted a lot of attention. 'I had more volunteers to engineer on Louise's record, and offers to work unpaid overtime in the studio, than I've ever had with another artist,' laughs Simon. 'I don't think Louise realises herself how attractive she is, but people are very, very interested in her. I even had people offering to work for nothing or carry bags, just so they could meet her.'

Despite the tell-tale signs of male interest, Louise remained oblivious to the attention she was generating within the male population. Instead, she was losing sleep, and weight, with worry about the imminent release of her début single, 'Light of my Life'. The week it came out, Louise was in a car when Denis called with the news of the mid-week chart position. 'I was so nervous and scared I kept saying to Denis, "Don't tell me, I don't want to know." But when he said the mid-week was number three I screamed my head off. I could have died, I was so happy.'

'I had been really worried that nobody would ever want to buy my records and that the fans would hate me for leaving.'

the sexiest woman in the world

Louise's first year as a solo artist was a heady and extreme mix of highs and lows. While the 21-year-old was still unsure as to how her solo career would be received by both the fans and the music industry, the first seal of approval came from the *Smash Hits* award ceremony in December 1995, where she was voted Most Fanciable Female. While nobody who has ever met Louise, and witnessed her obvious charm, was the slightest bit surprised by the accolade, Louise herself was flabbergasted.

'I was numbed by the news,' she says. 'I was so nervous about going up on stage because I thought everyone would be going: "Why has she won this award?". While I was collecting my award I realised my shirt button had come undone and I was so paranoid that people would think I'd done it on purpose to get attention. What made it even worse,' says Louise, still cringing with embarrassment at the recollection, 'is that my stylist, Bonnie, had put me in a black lacy bra of hers. It was so un-me.'

Overnight, Louise went from 'the sweet one' in Eternal to the horniest thing in the business, especially when she released the record that has gone on to become her trademark tune, 'Naked'. And while Louise trekked around Europe promoting the song, she became jinxed. For one Australian TV show she performed in two left shoes – one size six, one size four – after she picked up the wrong shoes from a store. A few weeks later, in Germany, Louise and her four dancers were performing at a record company showcase in new stage costumes. The blue-velvet trouser suits, however, weren't able to cope with the stretch and grind of their dance routines. During the last number,

'I was so nervous about going up on stage because I thought everyone would be going: "Why has she won this award?"'

Louise and her dancers heard simultaneous rips and, to their embarrassment, realised their trousers had split, leaving their bottoms exposed to the audience of record company executives.

Back on home ground, Louise's solo image was rapidly winning her a legion of new, and often male, fans. But Louise was struggling with the new demands of being a magazine cover girl. Being photographed by the likes of Mario Sorrenti (Kate Moss's ex-boyfriend, who shot her naked for the Calvin Klein campaign) was like nothing she'd ever experienced before.

'I knew I had to change my image, but I found it really hard to be "sexy". I'm not that sort of girl. I'm definitely not man-driven. I like women and would never want to alienate them. Anyway, I've always thought that being sexy comes from inside, not from how small your knickers are.'

Louise howls with laughter at the memory of the infamous *FHM* magazine shoot, where her smile landed her in "trouble". 'I was a complete novice at being "sexy". They kept telling me to stop smiling and pout, but I couldn't. Every time they brought out a sexy outfit for me to wear I'd say, "I'm not wearing that." I insisted on wearing my own clothes. I was so embarrassed.

'In the end, I looked about twelve years old in the pictures, so we had to do the shoot all over again a month later, and I had to meet them half-way with the sexy outfits,' Louise adds, 'It was an experience. Doing those pictures was quite an ego boost too, though not in a bad way. I was just so surprised that guys were interested in me. It was the first male interest I'd had in my life.'

The shoot was such a success that the magazine sold out on the stands and reprints were hurriedly ordered. All the while, Louise kept on attacking the charts, with hit after hit. Over the next year she notched up five top ten chart hits: 'Light of my Life', 'In Walked Love', 'Naked', 'Undivided Love' and 'One Kiss from Heaven'. Her album, *Naked*, débuted in the top ten.

'One Kiss from Heaven' was the last single to be released from the album, and Louise came up with an idea for the video. She enlisted the help of her closest mates: Sophie, Charlie, Michelle Gayle, Martine McCutcheon, Jamie Redknapp, Shane Lynch from Boyzone, Kelle, Shaun Maguire and MN8 to just chill with her while footage was shot of them all mucking about together. 'It was brilliant. I had the best day,' says Louise.

Inevitably, she had to capitalise on her solo triumphs with a five-week overseas tour to Thailand. But, determined not to repeat the loneliness she experienced with Eternal, she took Charlie along for company. 'I had always found bedtime the loneliest time of all when I was away, before,' remembers Louise. 'So Charlie would sleep in my bed with me. People thought it was a bit dodgy, two women sleeping together, but it definitely wasn't rock 'n' roll. We'd sit in bed together, watching TV and chatting over a mug of Ovaltine until we both drifted off to sleep.'

Despite feeling on top of the world, there were moments when things came crashing down on Louise, reminding her of the split from Eternal. Driving in her car one day, she was struck by a great new song, 'Power of Woman', which came on the radio. 'I said it was a bril-

'All the awards I've received have been great. But the best time for me – ever – was being voted Best Female Singer.'

liant song, then someone told me it was Eternal and I had to turn it off. I just couldn't listen,' she says. 'It wasn't that I was jealous, I've always been dead proud of their success, even after I left the group. It just brought back my painful memories.'

Those painful memories were to resurface when, at the 1996 *Smash Hits* Awards, Louise was waiting in the wings to perform after Eternal. 'I didn't want to watch them on stage because I got a lump in my throat just thinking about the girls. But I had no choice because I was on two numbers after them. Watching them perform really upset me, but in a good way. I just wanted to hug them all because I still do think the world of them.'

It was a night that Louise will never forget. Not only had she finally laid the ghost of her difficult split with Eternal to rest, but she was about to receive the ultimate vindication from the fans that proved all the heartache had, most definitely, been worth it.

Louise says the best moment in her life, and the one she will never forget, is standing backstage at the *Smash Hits* Awards ceremony and hearing the words: 'And the award for Best Female Singer goes to … Louise.' 'All the awards I've received have been great. But the best time for me – ever – was being voted Best Female Singer. It was the highlight of my life. It didn't just mean that people thought I looked nice, it meant they liked my work too. And that meant more than any-thing. I've always been ambitious, which comes as a surprise to people who don't really know me, and now that I have my solo career I really know where I want to go. To be honest it only really dawned on me how much I want from life when I went to see Michael Jackson at Wembley recently and I turned to my friends and said, "In five years time I'm going to fill this stadium." And I will. They just looked at me in astonishment and laughed, and I laughed too – but I will do it.

'It's not the singing, it's not the dancing; it's the performing. Nothing ever gives me the buzz that performing does. When I walk out on stage and say "Hi, I'm Lou", I feel a bit embarrassed to be out there in front of all those people. But then the music starts, something happens to me and I feel like a different person, I feel on top of the world.

'Even though I'm driven and work my hardest to get what I want from my career, I've come to the conclusion that I want my success in a way that makes me happy. You don't have to go to hell and tour for three years without a break, or go to countries you hate and not see your mum and not have a boyfriend. I think it's possible, if you do it correctly, and slowly, to build yourself – not as a machine, but as an artist.

'I do think, and hope, that my new album will take me in the right direction. It's something I'm really proud of. And to be honest, going out on tour for the first time on my own is going to be the highlight of 1997 for me.

'I'm just working towards the stage where I can sell music on the strength of the music alone. I want people to genuinely say "I like that song. Oh, it's Louise", rather than "Oh it's Louise, that bird in the papers with her bikini on". I'm not knocking that image, because in the past year it's helped to open me up to a new audience. But I don't want my career as a solo artist to be judged solely on what I look like. But, at the end of the day, if they don't, they don't. At least I know I've tried my hardest.

'After all the stresses and strains of the last two years, I've only now started to get my confidence back and feel good about myself. Of course, there are still things I'd like to change – like my footballer's legs – but I can honestly say I've never been happier and more at ease with myself than I am today.

'If anyone had said to me two years ago that I'd be sitting here now with a big smile on my face, I would never have believed them. Right now I feel the best I've ever felt in my life. It's taken a long time to get here and now I've arrived I ain't going nowhere.'

'I've always been ambitious, and now that I have my solo career I really know where I want to go.'

TO ALL MY FANS

I would like to thank everyone who has taken the time to buy this book and to support me throughout my career.

Every one of these pages is dedicated to you. I hope that you enjoy reading them as much as I enjoyed putting them together for you.

The creation of this book coincided with the recording of my new album and has been just as fulfilling – I really hope you like them both.

Thanks and more,

Love always
Louise x

DISCOGRAPHY

Release Date	Title	Highest Chart Position
25.9.95	Light Of My Life (single)	8
4.3.96	In Walked Love (single)	17
27.5.96	Naked (single)	5
24.6.96	Naked (album)	7
19.8.96	Undivided Love (single)	5
18.11.96	One Kiss From Heaven (single)	9
22.9.97	Arms Around The World	-
6.10.97	Woman In Me (album)	-

'SOFT AND GENTLE NO SWEAT TOUR' DATES

November 1997:

20th	Sheffield, City Hall
21st	Nottingham, Royal Centre
23rd	Portsmouth Guildhall
24th	Cardiff, St David's Hall
25th	Bristol, Colston Hall
27th	Liverpool, Empire
28th	Southport Theatre
30th	Aberdeen, Capitol

December 1997:

1st	Glasgow, The Clyde Auditorium
2nd	Newcastle City Hall
4th	Blackburn, King George's Hall
5th	York Barbican
7th/8th	Manchester Apollo
9th	Bradford, St George's Hall
11th/12th	Cambridge Corn Exchange
14th	Bournemouth International Centre
15th	Wembley Arena
16th	Brighton Centre
18th	Wolverhampton, Civic

AUTHORS ACKNOWLEDGEMENTS

Kate Thornton is a former Smash Hits editor and Daily Mirror columnist who currently works as a television presenter and freelance writer.
Jane Preston is a music and film writer who works for a variety of newspapers and magazines, including the Mail On Sunday and Premiere.

We would like to thank the following for their invaluable help in putting this book together; Oliver, Denis, Wendy, Cara, Karen, Becky, Lili at First Avenue for their faultless efficiency, Tim and Lynne Nurding for their time and happy memories, Sophie and Charlie for being so open honest and entertaining, Keith and Jed for disappearing at all the right times, Carolyn for being so calm, cool and collected and finally Louise, a true professional and one of the nicest people you could ever hope to meet. As always, it's been a pleasure.

PICTURE CREDITS

Paul Cox: 58, 59
Arunas Klupsas: 8, 15, 17, 25, 29, 33, 36, 38, 39, 45, 47, 51, 52, 53, 54, 57 centre, 63, 64
Randee St Nicholas: 18
Louise Nurding: 4, 7, 10, 13, 57 left
Victor Yuan: 1, 2, 3, 5, 9, 11, 14, 16, 19, 20, 22, 23, 27, 28, 31, 32, 35, 37, 41, 42, 43, 44, 46, 48, 49, 50, 55, 56, 57 right, 62

First published in 1997 by Virgin Books, an imprint of Virgin Publishing Ltd
332 Ladbroke Grove, London W10 5AH

Copyright © 1997 Louise Nurding
Text by Kate Thornton and Jane Preston
Copyright in design and layout © 1997 Virgin Publishing Ltd

A catalogue record is available for this book from the British Library
ISBN 0 7535 0205 4
Printed and bound by Butler & Tanner Ltd, Frome and London
Designed by Slatter-Anderson